GOING WITH THE
GRAIN!

GOING WITH THE GRAIN!

RECIPES USING QUINOA, FARRO, CHIA & MORE

This edition published by Parragon Books Ltd in 2014
LOVE FOOD is an imprint of Parragon Books Ltd

Parragon Books Ltd
Chartist House
15–17 Trim Street
Bath BA1 1HA, UK
www.parragon.com/lovefood

ISBN 978-1-4723-2985-1

Printed in China

New recipes, introduction and incidental text written by Christine McFadden
New photography by Noel Murphy
New home economy by Jane Lawrie
Additional design work by Geoff Borin
Internal illustrations by Julie Ingham and Nicola O'Byrne
Nutritional consultant: Judith Wills

Notes for the Reader
This book uses both metric and imperial measurements. Follow the same units of measurement throughout; do not mix metric and imperial. All spoon measurements are level: teaspoons are assumed to be 5 ml, and tablespoons are assumed to be 15 ml. Unless otherwise stated, milk is assumed to be full fat, eggs and individual vegetables are medium, and pepper is freshly ground black pepper. Unless otherwise stated, all root vegetables should be peeled prior to using.

Garnishes, decorations and serving suggestions are all optional and not necessarily included in the recipe ingredients or method. Any optional ingredients and seasoning to taste are not included in the nutritional analysis. The times given are an approximate guide only. Preparation times differ according to the techniques used by different people and the cooking times may also vary from those given. Optional ingredients, variations or serving suggestions have not been included in the time calculations.

Picture acknowledgements
The publisher would like to thank the following for the permission to reproduce copyright material: Cover illustrations courtesy of iStock.

CONTENTS

INTRODUCTION

Slowly but surely, grains have moved from the culinary sidelines to their rightful place as 21st-century food heroes. No longer dismissed as mere health foods, they have become must-have ingredients for chefs, they show up increasingly in food magazines and newspaper supplements, and are allocated ever-expanding shelf space in supermarkets. But what exactly are grains? Why all the hype?

Grains, or cereals (from Ceres, the Roman goddess of agriculture), are the seeds of cultivated grasses such as wheat, rice and barley. They contain the plant's embryo and with it a package of concentrated nutrients to support the new plant's growth. There are also so-called pseudo-grains, such as quinoa and amaranth. These are not grasses but share much of the same nutritional characteristics and culinary uses.

Grains are the go-getters of the plant world. They are not picky about where they grow and many positively thrive in scorching sun, sub-zero temperatures, and poor-quality soil. In prehistoric times, grains were one of the first foods that could be stored. They were key to transforming a nomadic society to one that put down roots, and are now a staple food for about half the world's population.

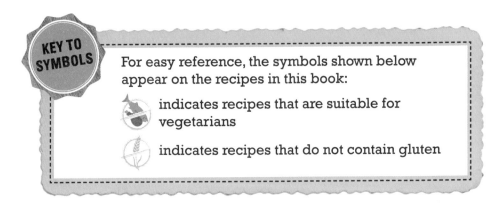

KEY TO SYMBOLS

For easy reference, the symbols shown below appear on the recipes in this book:

indicates recipes that are suitable for vegetarians

indicates recipes that do not contain gluten

RED RICE

ROASTED
BUCKWHEAT

FREEKEH

CHIA

QUINOA

PEARL BARLEY

AMARANTH

OATS

MILLET

SPELT

THE GRAINS

QUINOA (pronounced 'keen-wah')
Chenopodium quinoa

- - - - - - - - - - - - - - - - - - -

Quinoa is native to Peru and Bolivia where it was known as 'the golden grain' of the Incas. Botanically related to beets and spinach, it is one of the hardiest of plants, and trumps the nutrient content of all other grains. It is said to be the only plant food that contains all nine essential amino acids, putting it on a par with animal protein. It is also gluten-free. Not only are its nutritional credentials impeccable, it is also incredibly quick and easy to cook. Use it as a side dish and in a multitude of other dishes, including salads, soups, stews, stuffings, egg dishes, bread, cakes and desserts.

Shopping
Grains: minuscule white, red or black, round seeds with a pale band around the edge.
Flakes: use in the same way as oat flakes for a hot breakfast cereal.
Puffs: popped grains eaten as a breakfast cereal.
Flour: gluten-free, slightly bitter. Needs combining with other flours to make bread and cakes rise.

Cooking
• The seeds are naturally coated with bitter saponin that is removed during processing. The seeds should still be rinsed to remove any residue. Put in a fine-meshed sieve under running water and rub with your fingers.
• Use 1 part quinoa to 2 parts liquid.
• Put in a saucepan with the liquid and a little salt. Bring to the boil, then cover and simmer over a very low heat for 10 minutes. Remove from the heat but leave the pan covered for another 7 minutes to allow the seeds to swell. The band around the edge will uncurl like a spiral. Drain off any excess liquid through a fine-meshed sieve. Fluff up with a fork.

Tasting
The seeds have a mild, slightly grassy flavour and a unique texture – noticeably soft and light, but crunchy too. White seeds have a hint of sweetness while red seeds are slightly drier with a bit more crunch. Black are more intense flavour-wise with definite crunch.

AMARANTH
Amaranthus caudatus

Once the sacred food of the Aztecs, amaranth is a pseudo-grain that is botanically related to spinach and chard. It's a protein powerhouse, rich in calcium, gluten-free and highly digestible. Amaranth can be used in soups, stews, porridge, smoothies, desserts, bread and cakes.

Buckwheat, Mushrooms & Roasted Squash (p.92)

 **Shopping**
Grains: minuscule cream seeds.
Flour: gluten-free, slightly bitter. Needs combining with other flours to make bread and cakes rise.

 Cooking
• Soak for 8 hours, then drain and rinse before cooking.
• Use 1 part amaranth to 2 parts liquid.
• Put in a saucepan with the liquid and a little salt. Bring to the boil, then cover and simmer over a very low heat for 15–20 minutes. Remove from the heat but leave the pan covered for another 10–15 minutes to allow the seeds to swell. Fluff up with a fork.

Tasting
The seeds have an intense, earthy, almost corn-like flavour. The texture is somewhat gritty (soaking helps) and verges on gummy if left to rest.

BUCKWHEAT
Fagopyrum esculentum

Despite its name, buckwheat is no relation to wheat; it belongs to the same family as rhubarb, sorrel and dock. It is sold raw or ready-roasted. Roasted groats are often confusingly labelled with the Russian word 'kasha', but as far as Russian cooks are concerned, kasha can be any grain simmered in liquid.

Shopping
Raw groats: slightly bulbous, triangular, beige-green.
Ready-roasted groats: reddish-brown.
Flour: gluten-free. Use for anything from pancakes to pastry.
Japanese soba noodles: thin, brown, with a slightly rough texture. Sometimes made with a mixture of buckwheat and wheat flours so if you

are after pure buckwheat gluten-free noodles, be sure to check the label.

 Cooking

• Use 1 part buckwheat to 1½–2 parts liquid.
• Put in a saucepan with the liquid and a little salt. Bring to the boil, then cover and simmer over a very low heat for 10–15 minutes. Watch carefully as the groats soak up liquid and can easily turn to mush. Once tender but still chewy, drain off any excess liquid.

 Tasting

Raw groats: mild, slightly grassy.
Roasted groats: full-on earthy flavour.

Meatballs with Tomato Sauce (p.96)

CHIA
Salvia hispanica

Dubbed by devotees as the ultimate superfood, chia seeds were an Aztec staple thousands of years ago. The tiny seeds certainly pack a nutritional punch. They have the highest plant concentration of the omega-3 fatty acids and contain all the essential amino acids, plus a wealth of must-have vitamins and minerals. They are also gluten-free.

Eat the seeds raw, sprinkled over salads, soups, stir-fries and breakfast cereal, or add them to bread and cakes. They are more versatile when made into a flavourless gel to use in smoothies, chilled desserts, dressings or to bind meatballs and burgers.

🛒 **Shopping**

Seeds: minuscule white, brown, grey or black ovals.
Milled seeds: greyish powder used as a thickener.

Chia gel
Soak 1½ tbsp seeds in 125 ml/4 fl oz liquid for 15–30 minutes. Whisk every 5 minutes to prevent clumping. Cover and store in the refrigerator for up to 2 weeks.

 Tasting
Seeds are hard and crunchy with an unobtrusive nutty flavour.

FARRO
Triticum dicoccum

Farro is an ancient Italian variety of wheat, also known as emmer and often confused with spelt (*Triticum spelta*). Spearheaded by chefs and stylish restaurants, farro has enjoyed a well-deserved comeback in recent years. It works well as a side dish, or in soups, salads, stews and risotto (or *farrotto*, as it is correctly called in Italy).

🛒 Shopping
Whole grains: large, brown, oval.
Semi-pearled (*semi-perlato*): the bran layer has been scored to allow heat to penetrate more quickly.
Pearled (*perlato* or *dicocco*): the bran layer has been completely removed so the grains cook quickly.
Flour: low in gluten. Needs wheat flour to make bread and cakes rise.

🍲 Cooking
• Soaking is not necessary for semi-pearled and pearled farro, but can significantly reduce the cooking time for whole grains. Soak these for 8–16 hours, then drain. Rinse thoroughly regardless of whether it has been soaked.
• Put the grains and a little salt in a saucepan with plenty of water to cover. Bring to the boil, then cover and simmer over a very low heat for 10–50 minutes, depending on type and how tender you want it. Check the texture every 10 minutes. Once cooked, drain off any excess liquid.

Tasting
Farro has an intense nutty flavour. The grains are wonderfully plump with a satisfyingly chewy texture.

FREEKEH (pronounced 'free-ka')
Triticum durum

Highly esteemed in the Middle East, freekeh is becoming a must-have grain in the west. Made by burning young green durum wheat in the fields, freekeh has a unique smoky aroma and flavour. It contains more protein, vitamins and minerals than rice or ordinary wheat. The gluten content of freekeh is lower than that of regular durum wheat because the grains are picked unripe. However, freekeh is still wheat and contains gluten so should be avoided by both the wheat-intolerant and coeliacs. Use as a side dish or in risotto-like dishes, soups, stuffings and tagines.

🛒 Shopping
Whole grains: coarse, dark greenish-brown.
Cracked grains: lighter greenish-grey, irregularly shaped.

Spelt & Carrot Salad (p.70)

SPELT
Triticum spelta

Sometimes confused with farro (*Triticum dicoccum*), this ancient wheat variety has recently enjoyed an upturn. It is higher in protein and fibre than ordinary wheat, and may be less likely to cause bloating in susceptible people. Use as a side-dish or in risotto-like dishes, soups, stews and salads.

 Shopping

Whole grains: large, brownish-red.
Pearled: the bran layer has been scored to allow heat to penetrate more quickly.
Flour: easy to use. Makes bread dough rise more vigorously.

 Cooking
• Soaking is not necessary for pearled spelt but can reduce the cooking time for whole grains. Soak these for 8–16 hours, then drain. Rinse both types thoroughly.
• Put the grains and a little salt in a saucepan with plenty of water to cover. Bring to the boil, then cover and simmer over a very low heat for 10–50 minutes, depending on type of grain and how chewy or tender you want it. Check the texture every 10 minutes. Once cooked, drain off any excess liquid.

 Tasting
Spelt is rich, nutty and slightly sweet with a pleasantly creamy texture.

FREEKEH CONT.

 Cooking
• Swish the grains in a large bowl of water, discarding any chaff that floats to the top. Change the water several times, then drain in a sieve.
• Use 1 part freekeh to 2 parts liquid. Put the grains and a little salt in a saucepan with the liquid. Bring to the boil, then cover and simmer over a very low heat. Cracked grains need 25 minutes; whole grains need 45 minutes. Once tender but still chewy, drain off any excess liquid.

 Tasting
The grains are slightly crunchy with an enticing smoky flavour.

BARLEY
Hordeum vulgare

A multi-tasker in the kitchen, barley is hugely under-rated. It works well not just in homely soups, but also in stylish salads and risotto (or *orzotto* as it is known in Italy), breads and desserts.

 **Shopping**

Pot barley: beige grains with the bran intact.
Pearl barley: most or all of the bran removed.
Flour: low in gluten. Needs wheat flour to make bread and cakes rise.

 Cooking
• Rinse in several changes of water to remove dust.
• Soak pot barley for 4–8 hours before cooking.
• Use 1 part barley to 2½ parts liquid.
• Put in a saucepan with the liquid and a little salt. Bring to the boil, then cover and simmer over a very low heat. Cook pearl barley for 30–45 minutes; pot barley for at least 75 minutes. Drain off any excess liquid.

Tasting
Barley is satisfyingly chewy with a rich, earthy flavour.

MILLET
Panicum miliaceum/
Pennisetum glaucum

A long-term staple in western Africa and East Asia, millet is sadly under-appreciated in the west – no doubt because of its association with bird food. It is, in fact, one of the tastiest of the grains and is light-textured, versatile and very easy to cook. Use it as a side dish, as a stuffing and in salads, soups, stews and porridge.

Shopping
Grains: pale-yellow, small, bead-like.
Flour: gluten-free. Needs wheat flour to make bread and cakes rise.

Cooking
• Rinse in several changes of water, then drain.
• Bring a large saucepan of water to the boil. Add the millet and a little salt. For fluffy grains, simmer briskly for 10 minutes, then drain. Cook for longer for a porridge-like texture.

Tasting
Millet has a mild flavour and light creamy texture but still with some interesting crunch.

OATS
Avena sativa

- - - - - - - - - - - - - - - - -

A rugged grain that thrives in rugged conditions, oats are said to have their spiritual home in Scotland but Ireland lays claim to them too. Though theoretically gluten-free, they may be cross-contaminated with grains that aren't. If you are a coeliac, make sure you buy oats labelled 'gluten-free'. Oats are best-known for porridge, muesli and flapjacks, but they also make fortifying stews, tasty coatings, stuffings and toppings, and delicious desserts.

Shopping
Groats: pale-yellow. Need lengthy soaking and cooking.
Pinhead or steel-cut: groats chopped into pieces.
Flakes: pinhead or whole groats partially steamed and rolled to speed up cooking.

Cooking
Flakes: Use 1 part flakes to 6 parts water. Dry-fry for a few minutes to bring out the nutty flavour. Pour in the water and a little salt. Stir over a low–medium heat until boiling. Reduce the heat to low, then stir for 5 minutes, until thick and creamy.

Oat groats: Soak for 8 hours, then drain. Put in a saucepan with a little salt and plenty of water to cover. Bring to a boil, then simmer for 45–75 minutes.

Tasting
Oats are nutty, creamy and deeply comforting.

WHOLE-GRAIN RICE
Oryzia sativa

- - - - - - - - - - - - - - - - -

Since the bran and the germ are intact, whole-grain rice packs a greater nutritional punch than polished white rice. All types of rice are gluten-free.

Shopping
Brown long-grain: slim, elongated grains with a fluffy texture when cooked.
Brown short-grain: fat, dumpy grains that tend to cling together when cooked.
Brown basmati: super-slim, long grains that stay firm and separate when cooked.
Red: long, brownish-red grains with a white interior. Grains stay firm and separate when cooked.

Cooking
• An hour's soak can reduce the cooking time but is not essential.

- Use 1 part rice to 2 parts liquid. Reduce or increase this if you prefer a firmer or softer rice.
- Put the rice, liquid and a little salt in a saucepan. Bring to the boil and stir once. Cover tightly and simmer over a very low heat for 30–45 minutes, or until all the liquid has evaporated. Leave to stand off the heat for 5 minutes, then fluff up with a fork.
- Depending on the recipe, rice may be lightly fried before adding liquid.

 Tasting

Long- and short-grain brown rice have a nutty flavour and pleasantly chewy texture. Brown basmati rice has a distinctively floral aroma and a creamy texture. Red rice is intensely nutty, verging on meaty, with a chewy texture.

Khorasan, Banana & Walnut Bread (p.36)

KHORASAN
Triticum turgidum turanicum

Khorasan is an ancient variety of Egyptian wheat, which is often sold under the trademark KAMUT®. It is higher in protein and gluten than regular wheat. Use as a side dish or in soups, stews and salads.

 Shopping

Whole grains: impressively large, elongated, golden.
Flour: excellent for pasta-making. Imparts a rich, buttery flavour to bread and cakes.

 Cooking

- Soaking for 8 hours reduces the cooking time. Drain and rinse after soaking.
- Use 1 part khorasan to 3 parts liquid.
- Put the grains and a little salt in a saucepan with the liquid. Bring to the boil, then cover and simmer over a very low heat. Cook soaked grains for 30–40 minutes; unsoaked grains for about 1 hour. Once tender but still chewy, drain off any excess liquid.

 Tasting

The grains have a rich flavour, with pleasing chewiness.

BREAK THE FAST!

MIXED BERRY SMOOTHIE

SERVES: 4

PREP TIME: 10 MINS PLUS STANDING

COOK TIME: NONE

INGREDIENTS

1 tbsp chia seeds (preferably white)

375 ml/13 fl oz soya milk

125 g/4½ oz frozen mixed berries, slightly thawed, plus extra to decorate

1 ripe banana, sliced

3 ready-to-eat dried apricots, roughly chopped

2 tbsp honey

lemon juice, to taste

1. Put the chia seeds into a small bowl. Stir in 125 ml/4 fl oz of the soya milk and leave to soak for 15 minutes, whisking every 5 minutes to prevent the seeds from clumping together.

2. Put the remaining ingredients into a blender. Add the soaked chia seeds and their gel-like liquid.

3. Process for 1 minute, or until smooth. Pour into glasses and decorate with a few berries.

Soaked in liquid, chia seeds make a gel that can be used as a thickener in all sorts of recipes, including soups, stews and fillings for fruit tarts and pies. The gel will keep for up to 2 weeks in the refrigerator so it's worth making more than you need.

DRIED FRUIT COMPOTE WITH QUINOA

Quinoa takes on sweet, spicy, citrus flavours when simmered with honey, nutmeg and freshly grated orange rind. Adding freshly cooked dried fruit makes this a breakfast treat that is equally delicious as a dessert.

SERVES: 2

PREP TIME: 15 MINS PLUS STANDING

COOK TIME: 20 MINS

INGREDIENTS

75 g/2¾ oz white quinoa, rinsed

500 ml/18 fl oz water

2 tsp honey, plus extra to serve

pinch of freshly grated nutmeg

finely grated rind of 1 small orange

10 ready-to-eat dried apricots, halved

6 ready-to-eat prunes, stoned and halved

20 g/¾ oz dried apple rings, halved

4 tbsp dried cranberries

2 tbsp coconut chips

1. Put the quinoa into a medium-sized saucepan with 225 ml/8 fl oz of the water. Add the honey, nutmeg and half the orange rind.

2. Bring to the boil, then cover and simmer over a very low heat for 10 minutes, or until most of the liquid has evaporated. Remove from the heat, but leave the pan covered for a further 7 minutes to allow the grains to swell. Fluff up with a fork.

3. Meanwhile, put the apricots, prunes, apple rings and cranberries into a separate saucepan. Add the remaining water and orange rind.

4. Bring to the boil, then simmer over a medium heat for 4–5 minutes, until the fruit is soft. Drain, reserving the liquid.

5. Divide the quinoa between two bowls. Spoon the fruit over the top and pour over the cooking liquid.

6. Sprinkle with the coconut chips and serve immediately.

THREE-GRAIN PORRIDGE WITH RAISINS

Exceptionally rich in protein and gluten-free, this recipe is a nutritional powerhouse of quinoa flakes, oats and millet and makes an energy-boosting start to the day. Millet adds a nice crunchy texture to the creamy quinoa and oats.

SERVES: 4   **PREP TIME: 10 MINS**   **COOK TIME: 45 MINS**

INGREDIENTS

40 g/1½ oz gluten-free porridge oats

40 g/1½ oz quinoa flakes

40 g/1½ oz millet, rinsed

25 g/1 oz butter

850 ml/1½ pints water

pinch of salt

½ tsp ground cinnamon

¼ tsp vanilla extract

pinch of freshly grated nutmeg

90 g/3¼ oz raisins

milk or cream and soft light brown sugar, to serve

1. Put the oats, quinoa flakes, millet and butter into a heavy-based saucepan, preferably non-stick. Place over a medium heat and stir for a few minutes, until the butter has melted and the grains smell toasted.

2. Pour in the water, then add the salt, cinnamon, vanilla extract, nutmeg and raisins.

3. Bring to the boil, stirring constantly, over a low–medium heat. Reduce the heat and simmer gently for about 35 minutes, stirring frequently to prevent sticking, until the grains are tender but the millet still has some texture.

4. Divide between four bowls. Swirl in some milk, sprinkle with sugar to taste and serve immediately.

HERO TIPS Stir ice-cold cream or milk into the hot porridge just before you serve it, rather than while it is cooking, to enjoy the wonderful hot and cold sensations.

FRUITY PUFFED QUINOA

Quinoa puffs are a healthy alternative to regular breakfast cereal. Here, apple juice is used to moisten the puffs instead of the more commonly used milk. It makes a particularly refreshing start to the day, and is a good solution if you don't like milk on your cereal.

SERVES: 1

PREP TIME: 10 MINS PLUS STANDING

COOK TIME: NONE

INGREDIENTS

25 g/1 oz puffed quinoa
125 ml/4 fl oz apple juice
1 small banana, thinly sliced
½ crisp, red-skinned apple, sliced into thin segments
2 tsp pumpkin seeds
honey, for drizzling
Greek-style yogurt, to serve (optional)

1. Put the puffed quinoa into a serving bowl. Stir in the apple juice, making sure the puffs are submerged. Leave to stand for a few minutes.

2. Arrange the banana slices and apple segments on top of the quinoa.

3. Scatter over the pumpkin seeds and drizzle with a little honey. Serve immediately with yogurt, if using.

HERO TIPS

For a delicious variation, try using freshly squeezed orange juice instead of the apple juice. You could also replace the apples with pears.

QUINOA SCRAMBLED EGGS WITH CHIVES

Light and fluffy cooked white quinoa makes scrambled eggs even more satisfying and nutritious. For a superb flavour, it's well worth using very fresh organic or free-range eggs.

SERVES: 2 **PREP TIME: 5 MINS** **COOK TIME: 20 MINS PLUS STANDING**

INGREDIENTS

5 tbsp water
½ tbsp white quinoa, rinsed
4 large eggs
1½ tbsp snipped fresh chives
40 g/1½ oz butter
salt and pepper
sourdough toast, to serve

1. Put the water and quinoa into a small saucepan and bring to the boil over a medium heat. Reduce the heat, cover and simmer over a very low heat for 10 minutes, or until most of the liquid has evaporated. Remove from the heat, but leave the pan covered for a further 7 minutes to allow the grains to swell. Fluff up with a fork and set aside.

2. Lightly beat the eggs with the chives, adding salt and pepper to taste.

3. Melt the butter in a heavy-based frying pan over a low heat. Pour in the egg mixture and cook for about 2 minutes, stirring constantly with a wooden spoon, until the eggs are creamy but not yet solid.

4. Gently stir in the quinoa, then pile onto sourdough toast and serve immediately.

POTATO & ONION FRITTATA WITH QUINOA

SERVES: 4   **PREP TIME: 15 MINS**   **COOK TIME: 45 MINS**

INGREDIENTS

4 tbsp olive oil

2 large onions, halved and thinly sliced

125 ml/4 fl oz water

50 g/1¾ oz red quinoa, rinsed

700 g/1 lb 9 oz waxy potatoes, peeled, halved lengthways and thinly sliced

9 eggs

½ tsp dried oregano

½ tsp salt

¼ tsp pepper

1. Heat the oil in a frying pan, add the onions and gently fry over a low–medium heat for 25 minutes, until golden and very soft. Drain the onions, reserving the oil.

2. Meanwhile, put the water and quinoa into a small saucepan and bring to the boil. Cover and simmer over a very low heat for 10 minutes, or until most of the liquid has evaporated. Remove from the heat, but leave the pan covered for a further 10 minutes to allow the grains to swell. Fluff up with a fork.

3. While the quinoa is cooking, put the potatoes in a steamer and steam for 8 minutes, until just tender. Spread out to dry on a clean tea towel.

4. Beat the eggs with the oregano, salt and pepper. Stir the onions, potatoes and quinoa into the egg mixture.

5. Heat the reserved oil in a deep 25-cm/10-inch non-stick frying pan. Pour in the egg mixture, cover and cook over a low–medium heat for 15 minutes. Meanwhile, preheat the grill.

6. Place the pan under the preheated grill for 5 minutes to finish cooking the top of the frittata. Turn out onto a plate, cut into wedges and serve immediately.

RISE AND SHINE!

Breakfast styles vary, as do people. It can be on-the-run, or a peaceful sit-down occasion. It can be enjoyed solo or dished up to a hungry crowd. Flavours can be light and delicate, or big and bold. You may be the type who finds it difficult to get going unless you have had a decent breakfast, or you may feel daunted by the thought of eating so soon after waking up. Many of us think we don't have enough time for breakfast.

Whatever your attitude, a sustaining breakfast will kick-start your metabolism, help concentration and prevent that mid-morning energy dip. It can consist of anything you like, but the bare essentials are a whole grain, fresh fruit or a small pot of yogurt – or a combination. A bowl of fruit-and-yogurt-topped cereal or porridge, or a grain-based smoothie is refreshing, fortifying and quick to make.

Oats are the classic breakfast whole grain, but quinoa is one of the most versatile and easiest to eat. It is also the most nutritious – packed with protein, minerals and energy-giving B vitamins, and it's gluten-free. Quinoa puffs make the simplest of breakfasts – just pour some in a bowl, add milk or fruit juice and enjoy the crunch and pop. The flakes are also easy to use. Add them to muesli or cook them like oat

flakes in a comforting porridge. The cooked grains themselves are beautifully light and fluffy – delicious with fruit, honey and yogurt. They also lighten the texture of scrambled eggs and omelettes – stir them in as you cook the eggs.

Chia seeds are another healthy breakfast option. Sprinkle them raw over regular cereal or add to your favourite muesli mix. The seeds can also be soaked to make a flavourless gel (see page 10) that's handy to have in the refrigerator – whizzed up with frozen berries and yogurt, it makes a power-packed smoothie.

Pancakes are a favourite treat and perfect for a weekend brunch. For extra flavour and a more substantial texture, try adding nutty tasting buckwheat flour to the batter, or experiment with a mixture of quinoa flour and wholewheat flour.

Whatever your style, breakfast shouldn't be a chore. You need grab-and-go ingredients, or those that can be got going the night before – pancake batter or bread dough, for example. In terms of convenience, whole grains fit the bill. Puffs or flakes are ready for instant eating, and leftover cooked grains can be kept in the fridge for 24 hours (see page 88), ready to use in any number of tasty dishes.

BUCKWHEAT PANCAKES WITH RICOTTA

MAKES: 8   **PREP TIME: 20 MINS**   **COOK TIME: 15 MINS**

INGREDIENTS

3 eggs, separated

225 ml/8 fl oz buttermilk

1 tbsp melted butter, cooled slightly

75 g/2¾ oz buckwheat flour

55 g/2 oz plain flour

2 tsp baking powder

1 tsp caster sugar

¼ tsp salt

vegetable oil, for brushing

RICOTTA TOPPING

225 g/8 oz vegetarian ricotta cheese

1 tsp caster sugar

finely grated rind of 1 orange

1 piece stem ginger, finely chopped, plus syrup from the jar to serve

1. To make the topping, combine all the ingredients in a bowl, then set aside.

2. Whisk together the egg yolks, buttermilk and melted butter until well blended.

3. Combine the flours, baking powder, sugar and salt in a large bowl. Make a well in the centre and pour in the egg yolk mixture. Mix together with a fork, gradually drawing in the dry ingredients from the side until a smooth batter forms.

4. Whisk the egg whites in a large bowl until they hold stiff peaks. Using a metal spoon, fold one third of the egg white into the batter to loosen it, then fold in the remaining egg white.

5. Lightly brush a heavy-based frying pan with oil and place over a medium heat. Spoon in 4 tablespoons of the batter, spreading it into an 8–9-cm/3¼–3½-inch circle with the back of a metal spoon. Cook for 1½–2 minutes, or until craters appear on the surface. Turn and cook on the other side for 1½ minutes. Set aside and keep warm while you cook the remaining batter. Depending on the size of your pan, you can cook two or three pancakes at a time.

6. Spread the pancakes with the topping, drizzle over a little ginger syrup and serve immediately.

CHILLI & AMARANTH CORNBREAD

MAKES: 1 LOAF   **PREP TIME: 20 MINS**   **COOK TIME: 55 MINS PLUS COOLING**

INGREDIENTS

2–3 fresh red chillies, or to taste

90 g/3¼ oz amaranth flour

100 g/3½ oz gluten-free white flour mixture

115 g/4 oz coarse polenta (cornmeal)

1 tbsp gluten-free baking powder

1 tsp gluten-free bicarbonate of soda

1½ tsp salt

50 g/1¾ oz sugar

125 g/4½ oz vegetarian Cheddar cheese, coarsely grated

3 eggs

225 ml/8 fl oz buttermilk

70 g/2½ oz butter, melted and cooled slightly, plus extra for greasing

60 g/2¼ oz fresh or frozen sweetcorn kernels, thawed if frozen

1. Preheat the oven to 200°C/400°F/Gas Mark 6. Preheat the grill. Grease a 900-g/2-lb loaf tin.

2. Place the chillies under the preheated grill and cook, turning occasionally, for 5–7 minutes, until blackened all over. Remove the skins and seeds and finely chop the flesh.

3. Sift together the amaranth flour, white flour mixture, polenta, baking powder, bicarbonate of soda and salt into a large bowl. Stir in the sugar and cheese.

4. Whisk the eggs with the buttermilk and melted butter until well blended.

5. Make a well in the centre of the flour mixture and pour in the egg mixture. Mix together with a fork, gradually drawing in the dry ingredients from the side.

6. Stir in the chillies and sweetcorn and spoon the batter into the prepared tin, levelling the surface. Bake in the preheated oven for 40–45 minutes, until a skewer inserted into the centre comes out clean.

7. Leave to cool in the tin for 10 minutes, then turn out onto a wire rack and leave to cool completely.

KHORASAN, BANANA & WALNUT BREAD

MAKES: 1 LOAF

PREP TIME: 20 MINS

COOK TIME: 50 MINS PLUS COOLING

INGREDIENTS

4 small, ripe bananas

juice of 1 lemon

165 g/5¾ oz khorasan flour

1½ tsp baking powder

1 tsp mixed spice

½ tsp ground ginger

pinch of salt

85 g/3 oz unsalted butter, at room temperature, plus extra for greasing

100 g/3½ oz caster sugar

2 eggs, lightly beaten

50 g/1¾ oz walnut halves, roughly chopped

1. Preheat the oven to 180°C/350°F/Gas Mark 4. Grease a 900-g/2-lb loaf tin and line with baking paper.

2. Mash the bananas with the lemon juice to make a smooth pulp.

3. Sift together the flour, baking powder, mixed spice, ginger and salt into a bowl. Tip any bran remaining in the sieve into the bowl, mixing lightly with your fingers.

4. Put the butter and sugar into a large bowl and beat together for about 4 minutes, or until light and fluffy.

5. Gradually beat in the eggs and the flour mixture and fold in the bananas and walnuts, mixing evenly.

6. Spoon the batter into the prepared tin, levelling the surface. Bake in the preheated oven for 50 minutes, or until a skewer inserted into the centre comes out clean.

7. Leave to cool in the tin for 10 minutes, then turn out onto a wire rack and leave to cool completely.

CHOCOLATE, CRANBERRY & NUT MUFFINS

MAKES: 12 **PREP TIME: 25 MINS** **COOK TIME: 20 MINS PLUS COOLING**

INGREDIENTS

250 g/9 oz quinoa flour

2 tbsp gluten-free cocoa powder

2 tsp gluten-free baking powder

¾ tsp gluten-free bicarbonate of soda

½ tsp salt

125 g/4½ oz unsalted butter, at room temperature

125 g/4½ oz caster sugar

2 eggs, lightly beaten

1 tsp vanilla extract

finely grated rind of 1 large orange

225 ml/8 fl oz milk

125 g/4½ oz dried cranberries

50 g/1¾ oz macadamia nuts, roughly chopped

1. Preheat the oven to 200°C/400°F/Gas Mark 6. Place 12 paper muffin cases in a muffin tin.

2. Sift together the flour, cocoa powder, baking powder, bicarbonate of soda and salt into a bowl. Tip any bran remaining in the sieve into the bowl, mixing lightly with your fingers.

3. In a large bowl, beat together the butter and sugar for about 4 minutes, or until light and fluffy. Gradually beat in the eggs, vanilla extract and orange rind. Beat in the milk and the flour mixture, a little at a time, beating well after each addition. Fold in the cranberries and nuts.

4. Divide the mixture equally between the paper cases. Bake in the preheated oven for 15–20 minutes, until well risen and a skewer inserted into the centre comes out clean.

5. Transfer the muffins to a wire rack and leave to cool completely.

HERO TIPS

For extra flavour, mix a few chocolate chips into the batter. For a fancier version, top the muffins with cream cheese frosting or rich chocolate icing.

LET'S DO LUNCH!

SPICY TOMATO, TAMARIND & GINGER SOUP

Red quinoa goes beautifully with tomatoes, tamarind and ginger in this spicy soup. Known as *rasam* meaning 'essence', the soup is popular in southwest India, where it is usually made with chillies. Here, black pepper provides the heat instead.

SERVES: 4   **PREP TIME: 15 MINS**   **COOK TIME: 35 MINS PLUS STANDING**

INGREDIENTS

60 g/2¼ oz butter
1 small onion, diced
2-cm/¾-inch piece fresh ginger, finely chopped
1 tsp ground turmeric
2 tsp cumin seeds, crushed
¼ tsp salt
½ tsp pepper
400 g/14 oz canned chopped tomatoes
2 tsp tamarind paste
70 g/2½ oz red quinoa, rinsed
225 ml/8 fl oz gluten-free vegetable stock
4 tbsp chopped fresh coriander

1. Heat half the butter in a large saucepan. Add the onion and fry over a low–medium heat for 5 minutes, until translucent.

2. Add the ginger, turmeric, ½ teaspoon of the cumin seeds, the salt and pepper. Cook for a further minute.

3. Stir in the tomatoes, tamarind paste, quinoa and stock. Bring to the boil, then reduce the heat, cover and simmer for 25 minutes, stirring occasionally.

4. Remove from the heat and stir in the coriander. Leave to stand, covered, for 10 minutes.

5. Heat the remaining butter in a small frying pan over a medium–high heat. Add the remaining cumin seeds and sizzle for a few seconds. Swirl into the soup and serve immediately.

BLACK BEAN, SQUASH & SWEETCORN SOUP

This is a great Mexican-style soup, packed with strong, earthy flavours. A swirl of green-flecked coriander cream sets off the rich, dark colours of black beans and black quinoa. Served with gluten-free corn tortillas, it's a meal in itself.

SERVES: 6   **PREP TIME: 20 MINS**   **COOK TIME: 45 MINS**

INGREDIENTS

2 tbsp vegetable oil
1 red onion, diced
1 tsp dried oregano
225 g/8 oz (prepared weight) butternut squash, peeled, deseeded and cubed
400 g/14 oz canned chopped tomatoes
400 g/14 oz canned black beans, drained and rinsed
90 g/3¼ oz black quinoa, rinsed
600 ml/1 pint gluten-free vegetable stock
125 g/4½ oz frozen sweetcorn kernels
lime juice, to taste
salt and pepper

CORIANDER CREAM

175 ml/6 fl oz soured cream
6 tbsp chopped fresh coriander
salt and pepper

1. To make the coriander cream, mix together the soured cream and coriander, adding salt and pepper to taste. Chill until ready to use.

2. Heat the oil in a large saucepan. Add the onion and fry over a medium heat for 5 minutes.

3. Add the oregano and salt and pepper to taste. Cook for a further 2 minutes. Stir in the squash. Cover and cook for 5 minutes.

4. Add the tomatoes, beans, quinoa and stock. Bring to the boil, then reduce the heat, cover and simmer for 25 minutes, or until the quinoa grains have swollen.

5. Add the sweetcorn and simmer for a further 5 minutes.

6. Stir a good squeeze of lime juice into the soup. Taste and adjust the seasoning, adding salt and pepper if needed.

7. Ladle into six bowls and top each with a spoonful of the coriander cream.

3

4

5

FARRO & BORLOTTI BEAN SOUP

Farro is an ancient type of wheat grain that is similar to barley. Popular in Italy, it is used in all kinds of dishes – salads, soups, stews and rice dishes. Here it is combined with borlotti beans and pancetta in a hearty meal-in-a-bowl soup.

SERVES: 4-6   **PREP TIME: 15 MINS**   **COOK TIME: 40 MINS**

INGREDIENTS

115 g/4 oz quick-cook farro, rinsed

1 tbsp olive oil

1 tbsp finely chopped fresh rosemary

100 g/3½ oz pancetta, diced

1 onion, diced

2 celery sticks, diced

1 small red pepper, deseeded and diced

850 ml/1½ pints chicken stock

100 g/3½ oz canned, drained borlotti beans

4–6 slices ciabatta bread, toasted

salt and pepper

extra virgin olive oil and chopped fresh flat-leaf parsley, to garnish

1. Put the farro into a saucepan with water to cover. Add ½ teaspoon of salt, and bring to the boil. Reduce the heat and simmer for 10–12 minutes, until tender but still chewy. Drain, reserving the liquid.

2. Meanwhile, heat the olive oil with the rosemary in a large saucepan. Add the pancetta and onion and fry gently for 5 minutes, until the onion is translucent.

3. Add the celery and red pepper. Season to taste with salt and pepper and cook for a further 5 minutes. Pour in the stock, cover and simmer for 15 minutes, until the vegetables are tender.

4. Add the cooked farro and the beans. Cook for 15 minutes, uncovered, until thick and soupy. Add some of the reserved farro cooking liquid if the mixture becomes too thick.

5. Place a slice of bread in the base of four to six bowls. Ladle over the soup. Drizzle with extra virgin olive oil, sprinkle with parsley and serve.

BLACK BEAN & QUINOA BURRITOS

MAKES: 8

PREP TIME: 30 MINS

COOK TIME: 20 MINS PLUS STANDING

INGREDIENTS

60 g/2¼ oz red quinoa, rinsed

150 ml/5 fl oz water

2 tbsp vegetable oil

1 red onion, diced

1 fresh green chilli, deseeded and diced

1 small red pepper, deseeded and diced

400 g/14 oz canned black beans, drained and rinsed

juice of 1 lime

4 tbsp chopped fresh coriander

2 tomatoes

8 gluten-free corn tortillas, warmed

125 g/4½ oz vegetarian Cheddar cheese, coarsely grated

85 g/3 oz shredded cos lettuce

salt and pepper

1. Put the quinoa into a saucepan with the water. Bring to the boil, then cover and simmer over a very low heat for 15 minutes. Remove from the heat, but leave the pan covered for a further 5 minutes to allow the grains to swell. Fluff up with a fork and set aside.

2. Heat the oil in a frying pan. Fry half the onion, half the chilli and the red pepper until soft. Add the beans, quinoa and half the lime juice and coriander. Fry for a few minutes, then season to taste with salt and pepper.

3. Halve the tomatoes and scoop out the seeds. Add the seeds to the bean mixture. Dice the tomato flesh and place in a bowl with the remaining coriander, onion, chilli and lime juice, and salt to taste. Stir.

4. Place 5 tablespoons of the bean mixture on top of each tortilla. Sprinkle with the tomato salsa, cheese and lettuce. Fold the end and sides over the filling, roll up and serve immediately.

GROW TO IT!

Given the right conditions, almost any grain can be made to sprout. Two or three days of warmth, moisture and all-important rinsing will transform the dormant grains into super-nutritious sprouts that many people find easier to digest than the grain itself.

Used raw, sprouted grains make tasty fillings for sandwiches and wraps, and they add beautiful colour and crisp texture to salads and cooked dishes. Add them at the last minute so they retain their crispness. You can also cook sprouts in bread – just mix into the dough or batter before baking.

The most successful grains to sprout are quinoa and buckwheat. Chia seeds are easy to sprout too, though they take longer and the sprouting process is slightly different. Grains for sprouting must be whole – not hulled, cracked, pearled, split or roasted. This means you can't sprout roasted buckwheat or pearl barley, for example.

Sprouted grains are incredibly prolific. Just 2 tablespoons of quinoa seeds, for example, will produce about 8 tablespoons of sprouts, although the quantity will vary depending on the sprouting time, and the age and brand of seeds.

HOW TO SPROUT QUINOA

Quinoa sprouts are thin and soft, with an intense, woody flavour. They take about 2–4 days to grow and do best at an ambient temperature of 17–24°C/63–75°F. The following method will also work for larger grains, but you will need more water to cover them during the initial soak.

1. Put 5 tablespoons of white or red quinoa seeds in a shallow dish large enough to spread them out in a thin layer. Cover with 500 ml/18 fl oz filtered water or bottled still mineral water. Stir to make sure all the seeds are submerged.

2. Cover with clingfilm and leave to soak for 40 minutes.

3. Drain in a fine-meshed sieve and rinse thoroughly. Shake the sieve until the water stops dripping.

4. Tip the seeds back into the dish and spread them out again. Cover with clingfilm but leave a small opening for air. Leave to rest for 8 hours. Repeat the rinsing and resting three or four more times, depending on how long you want your sprouts.

5. Once the sprouts are to your liking, store them in the refrigerator and use within 24 hours.

DUCK & SPROUTED QUINOA WRAPS

MAKES: 2   **PREP TIME: 15 MINS**   **COOK TIME: 15 MINS PLUS STANDING**

INGREDIENTS

2 small boneless duck breasts, weighing about 375 g/13 oz in total

5 tbsp chilli jam

20 g/¾ oz wild rocket

2 soft wheat tortillas, warmed

4 tbsp quinoa sprouts (see pages 50–51)

4 spring onions, thinly sliced

salt and pepper

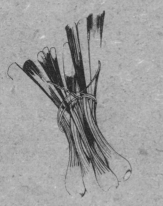

1. Preheat the oven to 220°C/425°F/Gas Mark 7.

2. Slash the skin on each duck breast diagonally in three places and rub with salt and pepper.

3. Heat a small, non-stick frying pan over a medium–high heat. Add the duck breasts, skin side down, and cook for 3 minutes without turning.

4. Transfer to a small roasting tin, skin side down, and roast in the preheated oven for 5 minutes. Turn over and roast on the other side for a further 5 minutes. Loosely cover with foil and leave to stand for 20 minutes.

5. Thinly slice each duck breast crossways into thin strips. Transfer to a dish and toss with the chilli jam.

6. Place a pile of rocket on top of each tortilla. Arrange the duck strips on top. Sprinkle with the quinoa sprouts and spring onions.

7. Fold up the bottom edge and sides of each tortilla and roll up. Serve immediately.

HERO TIPS

Don't worry if the duck breasts look pink when they come out of the oven – they will continue to cook whilst they rest.

QUINOA & SWEETCORN PAELLA WITH MINT

SERVES: 2   **PREP TIME: 15 MINS**   **COOK TIME: 20 MINS PLUS STANDING**

INGREDIENTS

135 g/4¾ oz white quinoa, rinsed

300 ml/10 fl oz water

2 tbsp olive oil

2–3 garlic cloves, chopped

2 fresh red or yellow chillies, deseeded and finely chopped

1 large tomato, peeled, deseeded and diced

2 tbsp fresh or frozen sweetcorn kernels, thawed if frozen

1 tbsp fresh mint leaves

salt

cos lettuce leaves, to serve

1. Put the quinoa into a saucepan with the water. Bring to the boil, then cover and simmer over a very low heat for 15 minutes. Remove from the heat, but leave the pan covered for a further 5 minutes to allow the grains to swell. Fluff up with a fork and set aside.

2. Meanwhile, heat the oil in a large frying pan, add the garlic and chillies and cook over a medium heat, stirring, for 2–3 minutes, or until the garlic is softened. Stir in the tomato and sweetcorn, heat until bubbling and cook for 1 minute.

3. Stir in the cooked quinoa and reheat gently. Taste and adjust the seasoning, adding salt if needed. Chop the mint leaves and stir into the mixture.

4. Serve with crisp cos lettuce leaves for scooping.

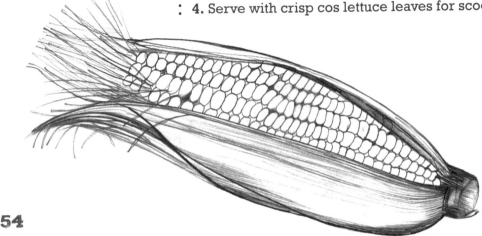

GREEN FARRO SALAD WITH FETA

A favourite in Italy, sweet and chewy farro makes a stylish salad with summery green vegetables and herbs, tangy feta cheese and a zesty lemon-oil dressing. The salad is just as suitable for a party buffet as it is for a summer lunch.

SERVES: 4

PREP TIME: 20 MINS PLUS STANDING

COOK TIME: 15 MINS PLUS COOLING

INGREDIENTS

225 g/8 oz quick-cook farro, rinsed

½ tsp salt

50 g/1¾ oz fresh peas

5 spring onions, some green included, thinly sliced

½ courgette, coarsely grated

35 g/1¼ oz baby spinach, shredded

4 tbsp chopped fresh mint leaves

4 tbsp chopped fresh flat-leaf parsley

85 g/3 oz vegetarian feta cheese, cubed

sumac or paprika, for sprinkling

DRESSING

2 tbsp lemon juice

6 tbsp extra virgin olive oil, plus extra for drizzling

salt and pepper

1. Put the farro and salt into a saucepan with water to cover. Bring to the boil, then reduce the heat, cover and simmer for 10 minutes, until tender but still chewy. Drain, then spread out on a tray to cool slightly. Tip into a serving bowl while still lukewarm.

2. To make the dressing, combine the lemon juice with salt and pepper to taste in a small bowl. Whisk in the oil. Pour over the farro and mix gently.

3. Stir in the peas, spring onions, courgette, spinach, mint and parsley. Leave to stand at room temperature for 30 minutes.

4. Divide the mixture between four plates. Arrange the cheese on top, sprinkle with a little sumac and drizzle with oil. Serve immediately.

MOZZARELLA SALAD WITH SPROUTED QUINOA

Packed with protein, vitamins and minerals, quinoa sprouts make this gorgeous summery salad a nutrient-rich meal. Be sure to use buffalo mozzarella rather than the ordinary kind. There is a world of difference in the flavour.

SERVES: 2 **PREP TIME: 15 MINS** **COOK TIME: NONE**

INGREDIENTS

- 25 g/1 oz watercress
- 200 g/7 oz drained vegetarian buffalo mozzarella, torn into bite-sized pieces
- 3 tbsp white quinoa sprouts (see pages 50–51)
- 6 radishes, thinly sliced
- 1 tbsp pumpkin seeds
- 6 Kalamata olives, halved and stoned
- ½ tbsp white wine vinegar
- 1½ tbsp extra virgin olive oil
- sea salt and pepper

1. Divide the watercress between two plates and pile the cheese on top. Spoon the sprouts over the cheese.

2. Scatter over the radishes, pumpkin seeds and olives.

3. Season to taste with a little sea salt and pepper.

4. Drizzle over the vinegar and oil. Serve immediately.

HERO TIPS

Instead of buffalo mozzarella you could use ricotta cheese rolled into small balls. It's important that the ricotta is firm and dry. If it seems wet, wrap in muslin and suspend over a bowl for 2 hours. Squeeze firmly to drain thoroughly.

CHICKEN, PAPAYA & AVOCADO SALAD

SERVES: 2   **PREP TIME: 20 MINS**   **COOK TIME: 10 MINS**

INGREDIENTS

2 boneless, skinless chicken breasts, weighing about 150 g/5½ oz each

2 tbsp olive oil

100 g/3½ oz peppery green salad leaves, such as rocket, mizuna, curly endive and watercress

1 large papaya, peeled, deseeded and thickly sliced

1 ripe avocado, peeled, stoned and thickly sliced

25 g/1 oz toasted hazelnuts, halved

2 tbsp red or white quinoa sprouts (see pages 50–51)

salt and pepper

DRESSING

2 tbsp lime juice

6 tbsp hazelnut oil

salt and pepper

1. Place the chicken breasts on a board. With the knife parallel to the board, slice each breast in half horizontally to make four fillets in total.

2. Place the fillets between two sheets of clingfilm and pound with a rolling pin to a thickness of about 8 mm/⅜ inch.

3. Heat the oil in a large frying pan. Add the chicken and fry over a medium–high heat for 3–4 minutes on each side, until golden on the outside and no longer pink in the middle. Transfer to a warmed plate and season to taste with salt and pepper.

4. Slice the chicken lengthways into 2 cm/¾ inch wide strips.

5. Divide the salad leaves between two plates. Arrange the chicken, papaya and avocado on top. Sprinkle with the hazelnuts and quinoa sprouts.

6. To make the dressing, whisk together all the ingredients until smooth and creamy. Pour over the salad and serve immediately.

QUINOA & WALNUT TABBOULEH

SERVES: 2　　　**PREP TIME: 20 MINS**　　　**COOK TIME: 20 MINS PLUS STANDING**

INGREDIENTS

100 g/3½ oz white quinoa, rinsed

250 ml/9 fl oz water

1 courgette, coarsely grated

2 large spring onions, thinly sliced diagonally

handful of fresh mint leaves, chopped

handful of fresh flat-leaf parsley leaves, chopped

8 walnut halves, chopped

DRESSING

3 tbsp extra virgin olive oil

1 tbsp lemon juice

1 tsp gluten-free Dijon mustard

1 garlic clove, crushed

pepper

1. Put the quinoa into a saucepan with the water. Bring to the boil, then cover and simmer over a very low heat for 15 minutes. Remove from the heat, but leave the pan covered for a further 5 minutes to allow the grains to swell. Fluff up with a fork.

2. Transfer the cooked quinoa to a bowl and add the courgette, spring onions, mint and parsley.

3. Mix together the ingredients for the dressing, then pour over the quinoa mixture. Stir gently until just combined.

4. Transfer to two plates and sprinkle with the walnuts. Serve at room temperature.

HERO TIPS

The high levels of polyunsaturated fats in walnuts mean that they go rancid easily. If possible, buy them with their shells on, store in the refrigerator and consume quickly.

QUINOA, GRAPE & ALMOND SALAD

SERVES: 2   **PREP TIME: 15 MINS**   **COOK TIME: 20 MINS PLUS STANDING**

INGREDIENTS

135 g/4¾ oz white quinoa, rinsed

300 ml/10 fl oz water

½ tsp salt

1½ tsp lemon juice

1½ tsp tamari (wheat-free soy sauce)

1½ tsp toasted sesame oil, plus extra for drizzling

85 g/3 oz mangetout,

150 g/5½ oz seedless black grapes, halved

2 tbsp almonds, halved lengthways

3 tbsp snipped fresh chives

2 Little Gem lettuces, leaves separated

white pepper

1. Put the quinoa into a saucepan with the water and salt. Bring to the boil, then reduce the heat, cover and simmer for 15 minutes. Remove from the heat, but leave the pan covered for a further 5 minutes to allow the grains to swell. Fluff up with a fork and set aside.

2. Whisk together the lemon juice, tamari, sesame oil and a little white pepper. Pour over the quinoa, and fluff up with a fork. Tip into a shallow dish and leave to cool.

3. Plunge the mangetout into a saucepan of boiling water for 30 seconds, then drain. Leave to dry, then slice each mangetout diagonally in two.

4. Carefully stir the mangetout, grapes, almonds and chives into the quinoa.

5. Arrange the lettuce leaves around the edges of two plates. Pile the quinoa mixture in the centre, drizzle over a little more sesame oil and serve.

THAI-STYLE TUNA SALAD WITH QUINOA

SERVES: 4　　**PREP TIME: 25 MINS**　　**COOK TIME: 30 MINS**

INGREDIENTS

60 g/2¼ oz red quinoa, rinsed

150 ml/5 fl oz water

4 small tuna steaks, about
125 g/4 oz each and
2 cm/¾ inch thick,
cut into thirds

2 tbsp vegetable oil

80 g/2¾ oz wild rocket

1 small cucumber,
halved lengthways and
thinly sliced diagonally

handful of fresh mint leaves

handful of fresh coriander leaves

3 tbsp dry-roasted peanuts

toasted sesame oil, for drizzling

SAUCE

2.5-cm/1-inch piece fresh ginger,
finely chopped

1 fresh red chilli, deseeded and
finely chopped

1 large garlic clove,
finely chopped

2 tbsp tamari (wheat-free
soy sauce)

1 tbsp gluten-free Thai fish sauce

3 tbsp lime juice

100 g/3½ oz palm sugar or soft
light brown sugar

1. To make the sauce, grind the ginger, chilli and garlic to a paste using a mortar and pestle. Scrape into a saucepan with the remaining sauce ingredients and cook, stirring, over a medium heat until the sugar is dissolved. Leave to simmer for 1–2 minutes, until syrupy. Remove from the heat and leave to cool.

2. Meanwhile, put the quinoa into a saucepan with the water. Bring to the boil, then cover and simmer over a low heat for 15 minutes. Remove from the heat, leaving the pan covered.

3. Put the tuna chunks into a dish. Add the sauce, turning to coat, then drain, reserving the sauce.

4. Heat the oil in a large frying pan. Add the tuna and fry over a high heat for 3 minutes, turning once. Transfer to a plate.

5. Pour the reserved sauce into the pan and boil for 3 minutes, until syrupy.

6. Combine the rocket, cucumber, mint and coriander, then divide between four plates. Fluff up the quinoa with a fork and scatter over the salad.

7. Arrange the tuna on top and pour over the sauce. Sprinkle with the peanuts and drizzle over a little sesame oil. Serve immediately.

RED QUINOA & CHICKPEA SALAD

SERVES: 4　　　**PREP TIME: 25 MINS**　　　**COOK TIME: 25 MINS PLUS STANDING**

INGREDIENTS

50 g/1¾ oz red quinoa, rinsed
125 ml/4 fl oz water
½ tsp salt
1 fresh red chilli, deseeded and finely chopped
8 spring onions, chopped
3 tbsp finely chopped fresh mint
30 g/1 oz gram flour
1 tsp ground cumin
½ tsp paprika
150 g/5½ oz canned chickpeas, drained and rinsed
1 tbsp vegetable oil

DRESSING

2 tbsp olive oil
2 tbsp lemon juice

1. Put the quinoa into a saucepan with the water and salt. Bring to the boil, then reduce the heat, cover and simmer for 15 minutes. Remove from the heat, but leave the pan covered for a further 5 minutes to allow the grains to swell. Fluff up with a fork and set aside.

2. Transfer the cooked quinoa to a large bowl with the chilli, spring onions and mint. Mix thoroughly.

3. Sift together the flour, cumin and paprika into a wide, deep bowl. Roll the chickpeas in the spiced flour.

4. Place the vegetable oil in a frying pan over a medium heat. Gently fry the chickpeas, stirring frequently, for 2–3 minutes, allowing them to brown in patches.

5. To make the dressing, combine the olive oil and lemon juice in a small bowl using a fork.

6. Stir the chickpeas into the quinoa mixture and quickly stir in the dressing. Serve warm or chilled.

HERO TIPS

Gram flour is made from ground dried chickpeas. It is pale yellow in colour, has a slightly nutty flavour and is gluten-free.

SPELT & CARROT SALAD

SERVES: 4

PREP TIME: 25 MINS PLUS STANDING

COOK TIME: 15 MINS

INGREDIENTS

225 g/8 oz pearled spelt, rinsed

½ tsp salt

2 tbsp fresh thyme leaves

40 g/1½ oz toasted pine nuts

5 spring onions, thinly sliced

4 carrots

3 tbsp salad cress, to serve

DRESSING

2 tbsp orange juice

1 tbsp lemon juice

2-cm/¾-inch piece fresh ginger, squeezed in a garlic press

2 tsp soy sauce

6 tbsp extra virgin olive oil

salt and pepper

1. Put the spelt and salt into a saucepan with plenty of water to cover. Bring to the boil, then reduce the heat, cover and simmer for 10 minutes, until tender but still chewy. Drain, then spread out on a tray to cool slightly. Tip into a serving bowl while still lukewarm.

2. To make the dressing, combine the orange juice, lemon juice and ginger juice in a small bowl. Add the soy sauce. Season to taste with salt and pepper. Whisk in the oil.

3. Pour the dressing over the spelt, mixing gently with a fork. Stir in the thyme, pine nuts and spring onions.

4. Using a vegetable peeler, shave the carrots into thin ribbons, discarding the woody core. Add to the spelt mixture.

5. Leave to stand at room temperature for 30 minutes to allow the flavours to develop. Sprinkle with the cress just before serving.

MONKFISH CEVICHE WITH RED QUINOA

Ceviche (from the Spanish *escabeche* meaning 'pickled fish') is made with raw fish 'cooked' in lemon or lime juice. Any firm-fleshed white fish can be used but it must be very, very fresh. Red quinoa adds appetizing colour and makes the dish more substantial.

SERVES: 4

PREP TIME: 25 MINS PLUS MARINATING

COOK TIME: 20 MINS PLUS STANDING

INGREDIENTS

450 g/1 lb monkfish fillets or other firm white fish, cubed

juice of 5–6 limes

60 g/2¼ oz red quinoa, rinsed

150 ml/5 fl oz water

4 tomatoes

1 red onion, diced

1–2 small fresh green jalapeño chillies, deseeded and diced

4 tbsp chopped fresh coriander

1 large, ripe avocado, peeled, stoned and cubed

extra virgin olive oil, for drizzling

salt and pepper

lime wedges, to garnish

1. Put the fish into a shallow, non-metallic dish. Pour over enough of the lime juice to cover and marinate in the refrigerator for 3 hours, stirring occasionally, until opaque. Drain the fish, discarding the juice.

2. Put the quinoa into a saucepan with the water. Bring to the boil, then reduce the heat, cover and simmer for 15 minutes. Remove from the heat, but leave the pan covered for a further 5 minutes to allow the grains to swell. Fluff up with a fork and set aside.

3. Halve the tomatoes and discard the seeds. Cut into small dice, and put into a bowl with the onion, chillies and coriander. Stir in the remaining lime juice. Sprinkle with salt and pepper to taste.

4. Divide the tomato mixture between four plates. Top with the fish and 2 tablespoons of the quinoa. (Reserve the remainder for use in another dish.) Scatter over the avocado.

5. Sprinkle with salt and drizzle with oil. Garnish with lime wedges and serve immediately.

ROASTED BEETROOT & BARLEY SALAD

INGREDIENTS

2 raw beetroots, peeled and quartered

3 fresh thyme sprigs

5 tbsp walnut oil

100 g/3½ oz pearl barley, rinsed

450 ml/16 fl oz water

1 large red pepper, halved lengthways and deseeded

25 g/1 oz walnut halves, roughly chopped

small handful of rocket leaves

thick balsamic vinegar, for drizzling

salt and pepper

1. Preheat the oven to 190°C/375°F/Gas Mark 5. Preheat the grill to high.

2. Divide the beetroots and thyme sprigs between two squares of aluminium foil. Sprinkle with a little of the oil and season to taste with salt and pepper. Wrap in a loose parcel, sealing the edges. Roast in the preheated oven for 30–40 minutes, or until just tender.

3. Meanwhile, put the barley into a saucepan with the water and ½ teaspoon of salt. Bring to the boil, then reduce the heat, cover and simmer for 35 minutes, until the grains are tender. Drain and tip into a dish.

4. While the barley is cooking, place the red pepper halves, cut-side down, on the grill pan and grill for 10 minutes, or until blackened. Cover with a tea towel and leave to stand for 10 minutes. Remove and discard the skin and chop the flesh.

5. Divide the cooked barley between four plates. Slice the beetroot quarters in half and arrange on top of the barley. Scatter over the red pepper, walnuts and rocket.

6. Drizzle with the remaining oil and some balsamic vinegar. Serve immediately.

WHAT'S FOR DINNER?

SQUASH, KALE & FARRO STEW

SERVES: 6   **PREP TIME: 30 MINS**   **COOK TIME: 55 MINS**

INGREDIENTS

1 dense-fleshed squash, such as Kabocha or Crown Prince, weighing about 1.25 kg/2 lb 12 oz

2 tbsp vegetable oil

1 onion, finely chopped

2 tsp dried oregano

2 garlic cloves, finely sliced

400 g/14 oz canned chopped tomatoes

700 ml/1¼ pints vegetable stock

125 g/4½ oz quick-cook farro, rinsed

250 g/9 oz kale, sliced into ribbons

400 g/14 oz canned chickpeas, drained and rinsed

6 tbsp chopped fresh coriander

juice of 1 lime

salt and pepper

1. Cut the squash into quarters, peel and deseed. Cut the flesh into large cubes (you will need about 650 g/1 lb 7 oz).

2. Heat the oil in a flameproof casserole or heavy-based saucepan. Add the onion and fry over a medium heat for 5 minutes, until translucent. Add the oregano and garlic and fry for 2 minutes.

3. Add the squash and cook, covered, for 10 minutes.

4. Add the tomatoes, stock and farro, cover and bring to the boil. Reduce the heat to a gentle simmer and cook for 20 minutes, stirring occasionally.

5. Add the kale and chickpeas. Cook for a further 15 minutes, or until the kale is just tender.

6. Season to taste with salt and pepper. Stir in the coriander and lime juice just before serving.

HERO TIPS

Use quick-cook farro (*farro dicocco*) so you can add it straight to the casserole without lengthy soaking or pre-cooking. It may seem as if there is too much stock, but once you add the farro most of it will be absorbed, resulting in a stew with just the right amount of liquid.

BARLEY & BUTTER BEANS WITH CHORIZO

Chorizo and red peppers add vibrant colour and flavour to homely pearl barley and butter beans. Use chorizo 'picante' if you want to spice up the flavour even more, or add a chopped chilli or two.

SERVES: 4   **PREP TIME: 15 MINS**   **COOK TIME: 1 HR 20 MINS**

INGREDIENTS

2 tbsp vegetable oil
1 onion, chopped
3 celery sticks, sliced
2 red peppers, deseeded and cut into squares
2 tbsp chopped fresh oregano
2 large garlic cloves, chopped
500 g/1 lb 2 oz chorizo sausage, thickly sliced
185 g/6½ oz pearl barley, rinsed
1 litre/1¾ pints hot chicken stock
400 g/14 oz canned butter beans, drained and rinsed
salt and pepper
steamed cabbage, to serve

1. Heat the oil in a flameproof casserole or heavy-based saucepan, add the onion and fry over a medium–high heat for 5 minutes.

2. Add the celery, red peppers, oregano and garlic and fry for a further 5 minutes.

3. Add the chorizo and fry for 5 minutes, turning frequently.

4. Stir in the barley and stock and season to taste with salt and pepper. Bring to the boil, then cover and simmer for about 1 hour, until the barley is tender but still slightly chewy.

5. Add the beans and simmer for 5 minutes to heat through. Serve with steamed cabbage.

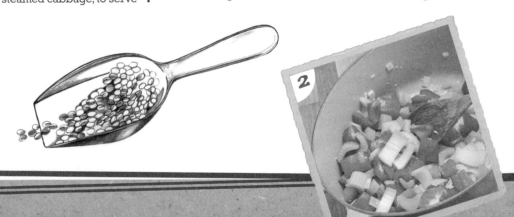

QUINOA & BEETROOT BURGERS

MAKES: 8   **PREP TIME: 35 MINS**   **COOK TIME: 1 HR 10 MINS**

INGREDIENTS

3–4 small beetroots, about 225 g/8 oz in total, peeled and cut into small cubes

135 g/4¾ oz quinoa, rinsed

350 ml/12 fl oz vegetable stock

½ small onion, grated

finely grated rind of ½ lemon

2 tsp cumin seeds

½ tsp salt

¼ tsp pepper

1 large egg white, lightly beaten

quinoa flour, for dusting

vegetable oil, for shallow-frying

slices of sourdough toast and peppery green salad leaves, to serve

WASABI BUTTER

1½ tsp wasabi powder

¾ tsp warm water

70 g/2½ oz butter, at room temperature

1. Cook the beetroots in a steamer for 1 hour.

2. Meanwhile, put the quinoa into a saucepan with the stock. Bring to the boil, then cover and simmer over a very low heat for 10 minutes. Remove from the heat, but leave the pan covered for a further 10 minutes to allow the grains to swell. Fluff up with a fork and spread out on a tray to dry.

3. To make the wasabi butter, mix together the wasabi powder and water. Mix with the butter and chill in the refrigerator.

4. Place the beetroots in a food processor and process until smooth. Tip into a bowl and mix with the quinoa, onion, lemon rind, cumin seeds, salt, pepper and egg white.

5. Divide the mixture into eight equal-sized portions and shape into burgers, each 15 mm/⅝ inch thick, firmly pressing the mixture together. Lightly dust with quinoa flour.

6. Heat a thin layer of oil in a non-stick frying pan. Add the burgers and fry over a medium–high heat, in batches if necessary, for 2 minutes on each side, turning carefully.

7. Place the burgers on the toast and serve with the wasabi butter and salad leaves.

QUINOA WITH ROASTED VEGETABLES

SERVES: 2   **PREP TIME: 20 MINS**   **COOK TIME: 30 MINS**

INGREDIENTS

2 peppers (any colour), deseeded and cut into chunks

1 large courgette, cut into chunks

1 small fennel bulb, cut into thin wedges

1 tbsp olive oil

2 tsp very finely chopped fresh rosemary

1 tsp chopped fresh thyme

100 g/3½ oz white quinoa, rinsed

350 ml/12 fl oz gluten-free vegetable stock

2 garlic cloves, crushed

3 tbsp chopped fresh flat-leaf parsley

40 g/1½ oz pine nuts, toasted

salt and pepper

1. Preheat the oven to 220°C/425°F/Gas Mark 7. Place the peppers, courgette and fennel in a roasting tin large enough to hold the vegetables in a single layer.

2. Drizzle the oil over the vegetables and scatter with the rosemary and thyme. Season well with salt and pepper and mix well with clean hands. Roast in the preheated oven for 25–30 minutes, until tender and lightly charred.

3. Meanwhile, put the quinoa into a saucepan with the stock and garlic. Bring to the boil, then cover and simmer over a very low heat for 10 minutes. Remove from the heat, but leave the pan covered for a further 7 minutes to allow the grains to swell. Fluff up with a fork.

4. Remove the vegetables from the oven. Tip the quinoa into the roasting tin. Add the parsley and pine nuts and toss together. Serve warm or cold.

HERO TIPS

You can use long-grain brown rice instead of the quinoa for a delicious variation on this dish. Make sure to adjust the cooking time accordingly – brown rice takes around 30–45 minutes to cook.

SALMON PARCELS WITH MILLET & SPINACH

SERVES: 4   **PREP TIME: 20 MINS**   **COOK TIME: 30 MINS**

INGREDIENTS

150 g/5½ oz millet, rinsed

4 salmon fillets, each about 175 g/6 oz and 3 cm/ 1¼ inches thick

15-cm/6-inch piece leek, cut into matchsticks

1 carrot, cut into matchsticks

1 celery stick, cut into matchsticks

1 tbsp snipped fresh chives

85 g/3 oz butter

200 g/7 oz baby spinach

salt and pepper

1. Preheat the oven to 220°C/425°F/Gas Mark 7 and place a baking tray inside. Cut out four 33-cm/ 13-inch squares of greaseproof paper.

2. Bring a saucepan of water to the boil. Add the millet and ½ teaspoon of salt. Bring back to the boil, then reduce the heat and simmer briskly for 10 minutes. Drain and set aside.

3. Place a salmon fillet in the centre of each greaseproof paper square. Arrange the leek, carrot and celery on top and sprinkle with the chives. Season to taste with salt and pepper and dot with half the butter. Roll up the edges of the paper securely, leaving room in the parcel for steam to circulate.

4. Place the parcels on the preheated baking tray and bake in the preheated oven for 12 minutes.

5. Meanwhile, heat the remaining butter in a frying pan over a medium–high heat. Stir in the reserved millet and the spinach and heat until the spinach has just wilted. Season to taste with salt and pepper.

6. Divide the millet and spinach between four plates and transfer the contents of one of the parcels on top of each. Serve immediately.

GRAIN TIPS

SHOPPING

No longer confined to healthfood shops, grains take pride of place in delis, farm shops, food halls and supermarkets, and they are easy to buy online. The choice is wide. The star of the show, quinoa, appears on the shelves almost everywhere, and more obscure grains, such as freekeh and millet, are gradually becoming mainstream.

If you buy packaged grains, always make sure they are well within the use-by date, and don't buy more than you are likely to need in that period. If you buy from shops where grains are sold in bins, make sure there is a good turnover.

STORING

Whole grains contain fat, and will therefore become rancid, although not immediately, if exposed to heat, light and air. Once you get them home, decant into airtight containers and store in a cool, dark place or in the refrigerator.

Once cooked, it is best to serve grains straightaway. If this isn't possible, they should be refrigerated within an hour of cooking and eaten within 24 hours.

COOKING

Grains need cooking in liquid to make them edible. Water is the usual choice, but for more flavour try using vegetable stock, diluted tomato juice or the water from cooked vegetables. Milk, coconut milk or fruit juice are other options. Adding a little salt will round out the flavour.

Remember that grains expand two to four times their size as they cook, so use a pan that allows for this. It should have a tight-fitting lid to keep in the steam, and a heavy base to prevent sticking. A wide pan is better than a tall one – grains need room to spread out and a large surface area allows the liquid to evaporate more quickly and the grains to cook evenly without becoming mushy.

VEGGING OUT

If you are a vegetarian, you need to balance your diet with a variety of foods. The bulk of these should be the starchy carbohydrate-rich type to give you energy, plus vegetables and fruit, moderate amounts of protein foods and a small amount of fat.

Whole grains are multi-taskers in this respect, providing most of the nutrients you need. The bulk of the grain (the endosperm) is made up of energy-rich carbohydrate and some protein. At its heart lies the fatty embryo or 'germ' that also contains protein. Surrounding both is the bran layer – another source of protein and fat, plus minerals, B vitamins, vitamin E and cholesterol-lowering fibre.

Compared with their highly processed counterparts – polished white rice, for example – whole grains contain more than the average amount of minerals and higher levels of most B vitamins, and some even provide 'complete' protein that's on a par with animal protein.

As the recipes in this book show, it's really easy to incorporate grains into a wide range of vegetarian snacks and meals. Just look out for the above symbol – this appears throughout this book to indicate which recipes are suitable for incorporating into a vegetarian diet.

GRILLED SEA BASS WITH FRIED QUINOA

SERVES: 2   **PREP TIME: 20 MINS**   **COOK TIME: 40 MINS PLUS STANDING**

INGREDIENTS

225 ml/8 fl oz water

85 g/3 oz white quinoa, rinsed

2 whole sea bass, about 350 g/12 oz each, scaled and gutted, heads removed

2 tsp fennel seeds, crushed

½ preserved lemon, roughly chopped

3 tbsp olive oil, plus extra for brushing

6 tbsp chopped fresh flat-leaf parsley

salt and pepper

lemon wedges, to garnish

1. Put the water and quinoa into a saucepan and bring to the boil. Cover and simmer over a very low heat for 10 minutes. Remove from the heat, but leave the pan covered for a further 10 minutes to allow the grains to swell. Fluff up with a fork and spread out on a tray to dry.

2. Make two slashes on each side of the fish. Combine the fennel seeds, preserved lemon, ¼ teaspoon of salt and ¼ teaspoon of pepper. Stuff the mixture into the slits.

3. Tip the quinoa into a 28–30-cm/11–12-inch frying pan. Place over a medium–high heat and sprinkle with the oil. Fry for 2 minutes, then reduce the heat to medium and cook for a further 15 minutes, stirring, until slightly crispy. Stir in the parsley and season to taste with salt and pepper. Set aside and keep warm until ready to serve.

4. Preheat the grill. Line a baking tray with aluminium foil. Brush the fish generously with oil and place on the prepared tray. Place under the preheated grill and cook for 4–5 minutes on each side, until the flesh is opaque.

5. Divide the quinoa between two plates. Place the fish on top, garnish with lemon wedges and serve immediately.

BUCKWHEAT, MUSHROOMS & ROASTED SQUASH

Roasted buckwheat is golden brown in colour and has a nuttier flavour than unroasted buckwheat. On its own it can taste quite plain, but mushrooms, onions and sweet-sharp balsamic-glazed squash provide this dish with appetizingly rich flavours.

SERVES: 4   **PREP TIME: 25 MINS**   **COOK TIME: 30 MINS**

INGREDIENTS

1 kg/2 lb 4 oz squash, such as Crown Prince or Kabocha

1 tbsp gluten-free thick balsamic vinegar

125 ml/4 fl oz olive oil

large knob of butter

225 g/8 oz roasted buckwheat, rinsed

1 egg, lightly beaten

450 ml/16 fl oz hot gluten-free vegetable stock

1 onion, halved and sliced

250 g/9 oz small chestnut mushrooms, quartered

2 tbsp lemon juice

6 tbsp chopped fresh flat-leaf parsley

25 g/1 oz walnut halves roughly chopped

salt and pepper

1. Preheat the oven to 200°C/400°F/Gas Mark 6. Cut the squash into eight wedges, peel and deseed.

2. Put the squash into a roasting tin and toss with the vinegar and 6 tablespoons of the oil. Season well with salt and pepper and dot with the butter. Roast in the preheated oven for 25–30 minutes, until slightly caramelised.

3. Meanwhile, put the buckwheat into a frying pan. Add the egg, stirring to coat the grains. Stir over a medium heat for 3 minutes, until the egg moisture has evaporated. Add the stock and ½ teaspoon of salt. Simmer for 9–10 minutes, until the grains are tender but not disintegrating. Remove from the heat.

4. Heat the remaining oil in a deep frying pan. Add the onion and fry over a medium heat for 10 minutes. Season to taste with salt and pepper. Add the mushrooms and fry for 5 minutes. Stir in the buckwheat, lemon juice and most of the parsley.

5. Transfer the buckwheat mixture to four plates and arrange the squash on top. Scatter over the walnuts and the remaining parsley. Serve.

2

3

4

QUINOA-STUFFED AUBERGINES

SERVES: 2   **PREP TIME: 15 MINS**   **COOK TIME: 45 MINS**

INGREDIENTS

2 aubergines (about 950 g/
2 lb 2 oz in total)

1 tbsp olive oil

1 small onion, diced

2 garlic cloves, finely chopped

135 g/4¾ oz white quinoa,
rinsed

350 ml/12 fl oz gluten-free
vegetable stock

1 tsp salt

pinch of pepper

2 tbsp flaked almonds, toasted

3 tbsp finely chopped
fresh mint

85 g/3 oz vegetarian feta
cheese, crumbled

1. Preheat the oven to 230°C/450°F/Gas Mark 8. Place the aubergines on a baking tray and bake in the preheated oven for 15 minutes, or until soft. Remove from the oven and leave to cool slightly.

2. Meanwhile, heat the oil in a large, heavy-based frying pan over a medium–high heat. Add the onion and garlic and cook, stirring occasionally, for about 5 minutes, or until soft. Add the quinoa, stock, salt and pepper.

3. Cut each aubergine in half lengthways and scoop out the flesh, leaving a 5 mm/¼ inch thick border inside the skin so they hold their shape.

4. Chop the aubergine flesh and stir it into the quinoa mixture in the frying pan. Reduce the heat to low–medium, cover and cook for about 15 minutes, or until the quinoa is cooked through. Remove from the heat and stir in the flaked almonds, 2 tablespoons of the mint and half the cheese.

5. Divide the quinoa mixture equally between the aubergine skins and top with the remaining cheese. Bake for about 10–15 minutes, or until the cheese is bubbling and beginning to brown. Garnish with the remaining mint and serve.

MEATBALLS WITH TOMATO SAUCE

Milled chia seeds are used here instead of breadcrumbs to bind the meatball mixture. The seeds develop a sticky gel-like texture when moistened, making them an excellent source of slow-release carbohydrates.

SERVES: 4   **PREP TIME: 25 MINS**   **COOK TIME: 45 MINS**

INGREDIENTS

800 g/1 lb 12 oz canned chopped tomatoes

5 garlic cloves, crushed

2 tsp dried oregano

150 ml/5 fl oz olive oil

½ tsp salt

chopped fresh flat-leaf parsley and freshly grated Parmesan cheese, to serve

MEATBALLS

1 small onion, grated

finely grated rind of 1 large lemon

2 garlic cloves, crushed

2 tsp dried oregano

1 tsp salt

¾ tsp pepper

1 large egg white, lightly beaten

500 g/1 lb 2 oz fresh pork mince

250 g/9 oz fresh beef mince

4 tbsp milled chia seeds

1. First, make the meatballs. Mix together the onion, lemon rind, garlic and oregano with the salt, pepper and egg white.

2. Combine the pork and beef in a large bowl. Add the egg white mixture, mixing together well. Mix in the chia seeds and leave to stand.

3. Meanwhile, put the tomatoes into a large pan with the garlic and oregano, 4 tablespoons of the oil and the salt. Bring to the boil, then simmer briskly, uncovered, for 30 minutes, until thickened.

4. Divide the meat mixture into 20 balls, rolling them in the palm of your hand until firm.

5. Heat the remaining oil in a large frying pan. Add the meatballs and fry for about 8 minutes, turning frequently, until brown all over. Transfer to kitchen paper to drain, then add to the sauce and simmer for 5 minutes.

6. Transfer the meatballs and sauce to plates, sprinkle with parsley and serve with Parmesan.

2

3

4

CHICKEN TAGINE WITH FREEKEH

SERVES: 4　　　　　**PREP TIME: 25 MINS**　　　**COOK TIME: 55 MINS**

INGREDIENTS

1 tsp harissa paste
1 tbsp cumin seeds
½ tsp pepper
1 tsp salt
125 ml/4 fl oz olive oil
1 kg/2 lb 4 oz mixed root vegetables, such as carrots, turnips and potatoes, peeled and cut into large chunks
8 chicken thighs, about 150 g/5½ oz each
2 onions, chopped
2 large garlic cloves, thinly sliced
150 ml/5 fl oz chicken stock
225 g/8 oz freekeh, rinsed
700 ml/1¼ pints water
6 tbsp chopped fresh coriander

1. Whisk together the harissa, cumin seeds, pepper, ½ teaspoon of the salt and 5 tablespoons of the oil. Pour half over the root vegetables and toss to coat. Rub the remainder into the chicken.

2. Heat 2 tablespoons of the remaining oil in a large flameproof casserole or heavy-based saucepan. Add the onions and gently fry for 5 minutes. Add the garlic and fry for a further 2 minutes. Add the vegetables, cover and fry for a further 10 minutes.

3. Heat the remaining oil in a frying pan. Add the chicken and cook, turning, for 6–8 minutes, until brown all over, then add to the vegetable mixture. Pour in the stock, cover and simmer for 30 minutes, or until the chicken is cooked through.

4. Meanwhile, put the freekeh into a saucepan with the water and the remaining salt. Bring to the boil, cover and simmer for 25 minutes.

5. Tip the chicken and vegetables into a colander set over a large bowl. Pour the drained juices back into the casserole and simmer for 5 minutes, until thickened.

6. Drain the freekeh and tip into a large serving dish. Arrange the chicken and vegetables on top, pour over the juices. Sprinkle with the coriander and serve immediately.

BUCKWHEAT NOODLES WITH MUSHROOMS

Also known as soba, these noodles make a satisfying super-nutritious dish when combined with exotic mushrooms, edamame beans and tasty seasonings. It's ideal for vegans and, if you use tamari (Japanese wheat-free soy sauce), it's gluten-free too.

SERVES: 4   **PREP TIME: 15 MINS**   **COOK TIME: 15 MINS**

INGREDIENTS

200 g/7 oz gluten-free buckwheat noodles, broken into short lengths

250 g/9 oz frozen edamame beans

5 tbsp vegetable oil

25 g/1 oz fresh ginger, peeled and finely chopped

50 g/1¾ oz leek from the green middle part, very thinly sliced lengthways

2 large garlic cloves, very thinly sliced lengthways

250 g/9 oz buna shimeji, mushrooms (or use sliced oyster or shiitake mushrooms)

½ tsp pepper

juice of ½ lime

3 tbsp tamari (wheat-free soy sauce)

TO SERVE

1 tbsp toasted sesame oil

2 tsp sesame seeds

25 g/1 oz pea shoots

gluten-free wasabi paste

1. Bring a large saucepan of water to the boil. Add the noodles, bring back to the boil and cook for about 6 minutes, until just tender. Drain, reserving the cooking water, rinse well and set aside.

2. Meanwhile, bring a separate saucepan of water to the boil, then add the beans. Bring back to the boil and cook for 3 minutes. Drain and keep warm.

3. Heat the vegetable oil in a wok or large frying pan. Add the ginger, leek and garlic and fry over a medium–high heat for 1 minute.

4. Discard the base of the mushroom clumps and separate the mushrooms. Add to the wok and fry for 3 minutes, until the mushrooms release their juices.

5. Add the pepper, lime juice and tamari. Cook for a further minute, then add the reserved beans.

6. Reheat the reserved cooking water. Add the noodles and swirl until hot, then divide between four bowls. Spoon the vegetable mixture over the top of the noodles. Sprinkle with the sesame oil and sesame seeds. Scatter over the pea shoots and serve immediately with wasabi paste for dipping.

GRILLED PRAWNS WITH CRISP-FRIED RED RICE

SERVES: 4

PREP TIME: 30 MINS PLUS MARINATING & SOAKING

COOK TIME: 1 HR

INGREDIENTS

500 g/1 lb 2 oz raw tiger prawns, peeled and deveined

juice of 4 limes

1 small fresh red chilli, deseeded and finely chopped

5 tbsp olive oil

125 g/4½ oz Camargue red rice, rinsed

300 ml/10 fl oz water

3 heads of red chicory, leaves separated

10–12 radishes, sliced

3 spring onions, shredded

4 tbsp red quinoa sprouts (see pages 50–51)

salt and pepper

1. Put the prawns into a shallow dish. Stir in the lime juice, chilli and 2 tablespoons of the oil. Leave to marinate in the refrigerator for 2 hours.

2. Put the rice into a saucepan with the water and ½ teaspoon of salt. Bring to the boil, then cover and simmer for 40 minutes. Fluff up with a fork and spread out on a tray to dry.

3. Meanwhile, soak four wooden skewers in a shallow dish of water for at least 30 minutes. Preheat the grill.

4. Tip the rice into a frying pan large enough to spread it out in a thin layer. Place over a medium–high heat and drizzle over the remaining oil. Fry for a few minutes until a crust forms. Turn and fry for a further few minutes. Keep warm over a low heat until ready to serve.

5. Meanwhile, drain the prawns, thread onto the soaked skewers and season to taste with salt and pepper. Place under the preheated grill and cook for 5–6 minutes, until pink all over.

6. Divide the chicory between four plates and top with the rice, radishes and spring onions.

7. Remove the prawns from the skewers and arrange on top of the salad. Sprinkle with the quinoa sprouts and serve immediately.

BABY SQUASH WITH FREEKEH STUFFING

SERVES: 4   **PREP TIME: 30 MINS**   **COOK TIME: 1 HR 10 MINS**

INGREDIENTS

115 g/4 oz freekeh, rinsed

350 ml/12 fl oz water

1½ tbsp tomato purée

4 round baby squash, about 10 cm/4 inches in diameter

3 tbsp olive oil, plus extra for oiling and drizzling

1 onion, finely chopped

2 garlic cloves, finely chopped

40 g/1½ oz walnut halves, roughly chopped

80 g/2¾ oz canned black beans, drained and rinsed

4 tbsp chopped fresh flat-leaf parsley

115 g/4 oz vegetarian halloumi cheese, sliced

salt and pepper

1. Put the freekeh into a saucepan with the water, tomato purée and ½ teaspoon of salt. Bring to the boil, cover and simmer for 25 minutes, then drain and set aside.

2. Preheat the oven to 200°C/400°F/Gas Mark 6. Lightly oil a roasting tin. Slice the top third off the squash and scoop out the seeds.

3. Heat the 3 tablespoons of oil in a frying pan, add the onion and fry over a medium heat for 3 minutes. Add the garlic, walnuts and beans and fry for a further 2 minutes. Tip into a bowl. Stir in the reserved freekeh and the parsley and season to taste with salt and pepper. Spoon the mixture into the squash, packing it in well.

4. Place the squash in the prepared tin. Cover the tin with a thick layer of aluminium foil, sealing well, and roast in the preheated oven for 30 minutes. Remove from the oven and increase the oven temperature to 220°C/425°F/Gas Mark 7.

5. Arrange the halloumi on top of the squash and drizzle with a little oil. Return to the oven and roast, uncovered, for a further 5–8 minutes, until the cheese is slightly browned. Serve immediately.

THREE-GRAIN PILAU WITH CHICKEN

SERVES: 4 **PREP TIME: 20 MINS** **COOK TIME: 1 HR 5 MINS**

INGREDIENTS

60 g/2¼ oz red quinoa, rinsed

50 g/1¾ oz Camargue red rice, rinsed

60 g/2¼ oz millet, rinsed several times

4 tbsp vegetable oil

1 red onion, finely chopped

3 celery sticks, finely sliced

3 carrots, coarsely grated

4 spring onions, some green included, thinly sliced

2 small skinless, boneless chicken breasts, thinly sliced

juice of 2 small oranges

55 g/2 oz dried cranberries

3 tbsp whole almonds, halved lengthways

salt and pepper

1. Put the quinoa and rice into separate saucepans with ½ teaspoon of salt and water to cover by about 15 mm/⅝ inch. Bring to the boil, then cover and gently simmer the quinoa for 10 minutes and the rice for 40 minutes. Remove from the heat and leave to stand, covered, for a further 5 minutes to allow the grains to swell. Fluff up with a fork.

2. Meanwhile, bring a large saucepan of water to the boil. Add the millet and ½ teaspoon of salt. Simmer briskly for 10 minutes, then drain and set aside.

3. Heat 2 tablespoons of the oil in a large, deep frying pan. Add the onion and gently fry for 5 minutes.

4. Add the celery, carrots and spring onions and fry for 2–3 minutes, until just tender. Season to taste with salt and pepper, remove from the pan and set aside.

5. Add the remaining oil to the pan and place over a medium–high heat. Add the chicken and fry until cooked through. Add the reserved quinoa, rice and millet and toss for 2 minutes.

6. Add the reserved vegetables, the orange juice, cranberries and almonds and toss with the grains until heated through. Serve immediately.

SWEET NOTHINGS

CREAMY COCONUT & MANGO QUINOA

SERVES: 4

PREP TIME: 15 MINS PLUS STANDING

COOK TIME: 20 MINS PLUS STANDING

INGREDIENTS

300 ml/10 fl oz canned coconut milk

115 g/4 oz white quinoa, rinsed

1 large ripe mango, about 550 g/1 lb 4 oz

75 g/2¾ oz caster sugar

juice of 1 large lime

4-cm/1½-inch piece fresh ginger, sliced into chunks

100 g/3½ oz blueberries

4 tbsp toasted coconut chips

4 lime wedges, to decorate

1. Put the coconut milk and quinoa into a small saucepan over a medium heat and bring to the boil. Reduce the heat, cover and simmer for 15–20 minutes, or until most of the liquid has evaporated. Remove from the heat, but leave the pan covered for a further 10 minutes to allow the grains to swell. Fluff up with a fork, tip into a bowl and leave to cool.

2. Meanwhile, peel the mango, discard the stone and roughly chop the flesh (you will need 350 g/ 12 oz). Put the mango into a food processor with the sugar and lime juice. Squeeze the ginger in a garlic press and add the juice to the mango mixture. Process for 30 seconds to make a smooth purée.

3. Mix the mango mixture into the cooled quinoa and leave to stand for 30 minutes.

4. Divide the mixture between four bowls and sprinkle with the blueberries and coconut chips. Decorate with lime wedges and serve.

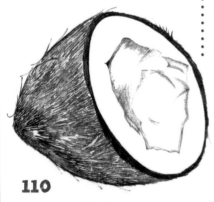

AMARANTH & BERRY DESSERT

SERVES: 4

PREP TIME: 10 MINS PLUS SOAKING & CHILLING

COOK TIME: 20 MINS PLUS STANDING

INGREDIENTS

90 g/3¼ oz amaranth, soaked overnight

225 ml/8 fl oz water

350 g/12 oz frozen mixed berries, such as blackberries, blackcurrants and raspberries, thawed

6 tbsp sugar, or to taste

lemon juice, to taste

whipped cream, to serve

1. Drain the amaranth through a fine sieve, then put it into a saucepan with the water. Bring to the boil, then cover and simmer over a low heat for 15 minutes. Remove from the heat, but leave the pan covered for a further 10 minutes to allow the grains to swell.

2. Meanwhile, put the berries and sugar into a saucepan, heat over a medium heat until almost boiling, then reduce the heat to low and simmer for 3–4 minutes, until soft.

3. Set aside half the berries. Put the remainder into a blender and purée until smooth.

4. Stir the purée into the amaranth with lemon juice to taste. Cover and chill in the refrigerator for 1 hour.

5. Divide the mixture between four bowls. Stir in the reserved berries, top each with a spoonful of cream and serve immediately.

HERO TIPS

Amaranth benefits from a thorough soak to soften its gritty texture. Overnight is a minimum but 24 hours is even better. Once the grains are cooked, it's important to leave time for them to swell before mixing with the fruit.

PLUM & HAZELNUT CRUMBLE

SERVES: 6 **PREP TIME: 15 MINS** **COOK TIME: 25 MINS**

INGREDIENTS

700 g/1 lb 9 oz ripe red plums
150 ml/5 fl oz water
75 g/2¾ oz sugar
4 thinly pared strips
of orange zest

CRUMBLE TOPPING

115 g/4 oz unsalted butter
115 g/4 oz quinoa flour
75 g/2¾ oz gluten-free
rolled oats
115 g/4 oz sugar
2 tsp vanilla extract
4 tbsp toasted hazelnuts,
chopped

1. Slice the plums in half lengthways. Separate the two halves and discard the stones. Slice in half again to make quarters.

2. Arrange the plums, skin-side up, in a single layer in the base of a 25 x 19-cm/10 x 7½ -inch baking dish.

3. Put the water, sugar and orange zest into a small saucepan, bring to the boil and boil for about 5 minutes, or until syrupy. Remove and discard the orange zest. Pour the syrup over the plums.

4. Preheat the oven to 190°C/375°F/Gas Mark 5. To make the crumble topping, rub the butter into the flour. Add the remaining ingredients and mix to form a crumbly dough. Add 1 tablespoon of water if the mixture seems too dry.

5. Scatter the crumble topping evenly over the plums. Bake in the preheated oven for 20 minutes, until the juices are bubbling and the plums are cooked through. Cover with foil if the topping starts to brown too quickly. Remove from the oven, spoon the crumble into bowls and serve immediately.

3

4

5

BETTER BAKES

If you enjoy baking, you'll have fun experimenting with wholegrain flours. As well as wholewheat flour, there are less familiar ones, such as millet or buckwheat flours, and those made with pseudo-grains, such as quinoa and amaranth. They provide extra nutrients as well as interesting textures and flavours, and can all be used successfully to make moist cakes, crisp biscuits and pastry, and tasty bread.

GLUTEN

Flour is categorised in terms of its 'strength', which in turn is a measure of its gluten content. Gluten is a type of protein contained in the starchy part of the grain. When kneaded with water and yeast it helps produce an elastic, aerated dough that rises well and holds together when cooked.

Although it produces superior dough, gluten can also cause serious sensitivity known as coeliac disease, and sufferers must follow a gluten-free diet. Fortunately, several of the wholegrain flours are gluten-free, and there are an increasing number of gluten-free flour mixes on the market, together with products such as xanthan gum and guar gum that thicken and emulsify gluten-free ingredients. The chart on the opposite page shows which grains can be consumed safely by those following a gluten-free diet.

Wholegrain flours that are low in gluten or completely gluten-free, need treating a little differently to regular wheat flour to lighten the texture of pastry and cakes. They can either be combined with a high-gluten flour, or given a boost with a raising agent, such as buttermilk, bicarbonate of soda or baking powder (the latter may contain a form of wheat starch so, if you need to avoid gluten, check the label before use). They usually need more liquid to be added and benefit from a resting period after kneading to allow the bran to soften.

	Contains gluten	Gluten-free
Amaranth		✓
Barley	✓	
Buckwheat		✓
Chia		✓
Cornmeal		✓
Farro	✓	
Freekeh	✓	
Khorasan	✓	
Millet		✓
Oats*		✓
Quinoa		✓
Rice		✓
Rye	✓	
Spelt	✓	

*Oats are theoretically gluten-free but may be cross-contaminated during growing, harvesting or processing with grains that are not. Look for oats labelled 'gluten-free' on the pack.

HUMIDITY

The amount of moisture in the air will affect your bread or pastry dough. When the air is damp you may need to add less liquid, and vice versa on hot, dry days or even on bone-chilling days when the central heating is blasting. Experience will tell you when dough feels 'just right'. If it's too sticky or too dry, just sprinkle with a little flour or water and gradually work it in.

STORING

Wholegrain flours last for months if stored in airtight containers in a cool, dark place. If you haven't used the flour for a while, smell or taste a pinch before using it. It shouldn't be musty or rancid.

APRICOT & RAISIN OAT BARS

Perfect if you're counting calories, these fibre-rich cereal bars contain almost no fat but have lots of flavour and are moist and chewy. They will keep for over a week in a sealed plastic container, so it's worth making a double batch.

MAKES: 12 BARS   **PREP TIME: 15 MINS**   **COOK TIME: 45 MINS PLUS COOLING**

INGREDIENTS

350 g/12 oz ready-to-eat dried apricots

2 tbsp sunflower oil, plus extra for oiling

finely grated rind of ½ orange

seeds from 5 cardamom pods, crushed (optional)

140 g/5 oz raisins

115 g/4 oz gluten-free rolled oats

1. Put the apricots into a saucepan with enough water to cover. Heat over a medium heat until almost boiling, then reduce the heat and simmer for 5 minutes, or until completely soft. Drain.

2. Put the apricots into a food processor with the 2 tablespoons of oil and purée.

3. Tip the purée into a bowl and stir in the orange rind and the cardamom seeds, if using. Leave to cool.

4. Preheat the oven to 180°C/350°F/Gas Mark 4. Brush a 20-cm/8-inch square baking tin with oil.

5. Stir the raisins and oats into the apricot mixture.

6. Spread out the mixture in the prepared tin, levelling the surface with a spatula. Bake in the preheated oven for 35–40 minutes, until firm. Cover with foil after about 25 minutes to prevent burning.

7. Leave to cool in the tin for 15 minutes. Turn out onto a wire rack and leave to cool completely before cutting into bars.

HONEY & BLUEBERRY CRUNCH BARS

MAKES: 12 BARS

PREP TIME: 15 MINS

COOK TIME: 30 MINS PLUS COOLING

INGREDIENTS

sunflower oil, for oiling

85 g/3 oz gluten-free self-raising flour

55 g/2 oz quinoa flakes

55 g/2 oz puffed rice

55 g/2 oz flaked almonds

225 g/8 oz blueberries

100 g/3½ oz dairy-free spread

100 g/3½ oz honey

1 egg, beaten

1. Preheat the oven to 180°C/350°F/Gas Mark 4. Brush a shallow 28 x 18-cm/11 x 7-inch baking tin with oil and line the base with baking paper.

2. Mix together the flour, quinoa, puffed rice, almonds and blueberries. Place the spread and honey in a pan and heat gently until melted, then stir evenly into the dry ingredients with the egg.

3. Spread out the mixture in the prepared tin, levelling the surface with a spatula. Bake in the preheated oven for 25–30 minutes, until golden brown and firm.

4. Leave to cool in the tin for 15 minutes, and cut into 12 bars. Transfer to a wire rack to cool completely.

WALNUT & CHOCOLATE TART

SERVES: 8-10

PREP TIME: 35 MINS PLUS CHILLING

COOK TIME: 45 MINS PLUS COOLING

INGREDIENTS

250 g/9 oz walnut pieces

175 g/6 oz caster sugar

3 eggs

60 g/2¼ oz amaretti biscuits, roughly crushed

55 g/2 oz unsalted butter, melted, plus extra for greasing

85 g/3 oz plain chocolate, at least 85% cocoa solids, melted

1 tbsp instant coffee granules

BUCKWHEAT PASTRY

115 g/4 oz buckwheat flour

70 g/2½ oz plain white flour

1 tbsp cocoa powder

2 tbsp sugar

115 g/4 oz unsalted butter

1½ tbsp chilled water

1. To make the pastry, sift the flours, cocoa powder and sugar into a large bowl. Rub in the butter with your fingertips until the mixture resembles breadcrumbs. Mix in the water with a fork. Knead lightly, then wrap in clingfilm and chill for 30 minutes.

2. Preheat the oven to 160°C/325°F/Gas Mark 3. Grease a deep 24-cm/9½-inch round tart tin.

3. Roll the pastry into a round and use to line the tin. Trim the edges with a rolling pin.

4. Put 225 g/8 oz of the walnuts and 55 g/2 oz of the sugar into a food processor and grind to a powder.

5. Beat together the remaining sugar and the eggs for 5 minutes, until thick. Beat in the walnut mixture, followed by the amaretti biscuits, butter, chocolate and coffee granules.

6. Spoon into the pastry case and bake in the preheated oven for 35 minutes. Remove from the oven (do not switch off the oven) and decorate with the remaining walnuts. Return to the oven and bake for a further 10 minutes, or until a skewer inserted into the centre comes out clean.

7. Leave to cool in the tin for 15 minutes before turning out.

SPICY SQUASH CAKE

SERVES: 8

PREP TIME: 30 MINS PLUS SOAKING

COOK TIME: 1 HR 15 MINS PLUS COOLING

INGREDIENTS

50 g/1¾ oz sultanas

450 g/1 lb butternut squash, peeled, deseeded and diced (prepared weight)

150 g/5½ oz unsalted butter, plus extra for greasing

150 g/5½ oz caster sugar

50 g/1¾ oz almonds, chopped

50 g/1¾ oz Italian mixed peel

finely grated rind of 1 lemon

1½ tsp ground cinnamon

1½ tsp ground ginger

85 g/3 oz khorasan flour

1 heaped tsp baking powder

2 eggs, separated

icing sugar, for dusting

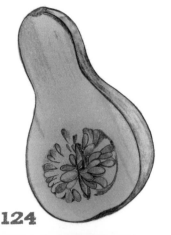

1. Put the sultanas into a bowl, pour over boiling water to cover and leave to soak.

2. Preheat the oven to 180°C/350°F/Gas Mark 4. Grease and line a 23-cm/9-inch springform cake tin.

3. Put the squash and butter into a saucepan. Cover and cook over a medium heat for about 15 minutes, until soft. Tip into a bowl and beat until smooth.

4. Stir in the sugar, almonds, mixed peel, lemon rind, cinnamon, ginger and sultanas, mixing well.

5. Sift together the flour and baking powder, tipping any bran remaining in the sieve into the bowl. Gradually beat into the squash mixture.

6. Beat the egg yolks for about 3 minutes, until thick. Fold into the squash mixture.

7. Whisk the egg whites until they hold stiff peaks. Fold carefully into the mixture using a large metal spoon. Spoon the batter into the prepared tin.

8. Bake in the preheated oven for 1 hour, or until a skewer inserted into the centre comes out clean. Turn out onto a wire rack to cool. Dust with icing sugar just before serving.

CLEMENTINE ALMOND CAKE

SERVES: 8-10   **PREP TIME: 30 MINS**   **COOK TIME: 40 MINS PLUS COOLING**

INGREDIENTS

125 g/4½ oz unsalted butter, plus extra for greasing
125 g/4½ oz caster sugar
4 eggs, separated
150 g/5½ oz millet flour
2 tsp gluten-free baking powder
125 g/4½ oz ground almonds
juice and finely grated rind of 2 clementines

SYRUP

juice of 4 clementines
100 g/3½ oz caster sugar

TOPPING

225 g/8 oz vegetarian low-fat soft curd cheese or quark
2 tbsp sugar
2 tbsp extra-thick double cream

1. Preheat the oven to 180°C/350°F/Gas Mark 4. Grease a 23-cm/9-inch springform cake tin.

2. Beat together the butter and sugar for 3 minutes, until fluffy. Gradually beat in the egg yolks.

3. Combine the flour, baking powder and ground almonds, then beat into the butter, sugar and egg yolk mixture. Mix in the clementine juice, reserving the rind.

4. Whisk the egg whites until they hold stiff peaks. Fold carefully into the mixture using a large metal spoon. Spoon the batter into the prepared tin.

5. Bake in the preheated oven for 30–40 minutes, until a skewer inserted into the centre comes out clean.

6. Meanwhile, to make the syrup, put the clementine juice and sugar into a small saucepan, bring to the boil and boil for 3 minutes, until syrupy.

7. Make holes all over the surface of the cake with a skewer. Pour over the hot syrup. When it has trickled into the holes, remove from the tin and transfer to a wire rack to cool completely.

8. To make the topping, beat together the curd cheese, sugar and cream. Spread over the cake and sprinkle with the reserved clementine rind.

INDEX